Reading for Eve... Phonics

Grade 3

by
Linda Armstrong

Published by Instructional Fair
an imprint of
Frank Schaffer Publications®

Instructional Fair

Author: Linda Armstrong
Editor: Krista Fanning
Interior Designer: Lori Kibbey
Interior Artist: Marty Bucella

Frank Schaffer Publications®

Instructional Fair is an imprint of Frank Schaffer Publications.

Send all inquiries to:
Frank Schaffer Publications
3195 Wilson Drive NW
Grand Rapids, Michigan 49534

Reading for Every Child: Phonics—grade 3

ISBN: 0-7424-2833-8

3 4 5 6 7 8 9 10 MAZ 10 09 08 07

Table of Contents

Reading First

The Reading First program is part of the No Child Left Behind Act. This program is based on research by the National Reading Panel that identifies five key areas for early reading instruction—phonemic awareness, phonics, fluency, vocabulary, and comprehension.

Phonemic Awareness

Phonemic awareness focuses on a child's understanding of letter sounds and the ability to manipulate those sounds. Listening is a crucial component, as the emphasis at this level is on sounds that are heard and differentiated in each word the child hears.

Phonics

After students recognize sounds that make up words, they must then connect those sounds to *written* text. An important part of phonics instruction is systematic encounters with letters and letter combinations.

Fluency

Fluent readers are able to recognize words quickly. They are able to read aloud with expression and do not stumble over words. The goal of fluency is to read more smoothly and with *comprehension*.

Vocabulary

In order to understand what they read, students must first have a solid base of vocabulary words. As students increase their vocabulary knowledge, they also increase their comprehension and fluency.

Comprehension

Comprehension is "putting it all together" to understand what has been read. With both fiction and nonfiction texts, students become active readers as they learn to use specific comprehension strategies before, during, and after reading.

About This Book

Learning to read is a complex process involving many interrelated skills. Supporting current state standards, *Reading for Every Child: Phonics* is designed to help students become proficient readers. As they complete reproducible worksheets in this book, students will review basic vowel and consonant sounds. Through puzzle solving, classification exercises, and context challenges, students will expand their knowledge of consonant blends, digraphs, diphthongs, special vowel sounds, and irregular forms.

While enjoying the activities in this book, young readers will unlock the power of structural clues. They will break daunting polysyllabic compound words into familiar components. They will learn to recognize syllables—a skill which will help them decode long, unfamiliar strings of text. Learning more about plurals and inflectional endings will also help them recognize and understand hundreds of additional words.

Your third graders will expand both their reading and oral vocabularies while learning prefixes, suffixes, and root words. They will start to recognize complex words in the chapter books and junior novels you read aloud and in the increasingly difficult stories they read independently. Also in this book, students will work with analogies, a skill that stretches many cognitive abilities. They will practice homophones, homographs, synonyms, antonyms, contractions, and possessives as well.

Students will have opportunities to practice alphabetizing words up to the second letter, an important dictionary and reference skill. Encourage them to find the meanings of words they encounter in social studies and science texts, as well as in fiction. The simple habit of looking up words and information is a skill with real-life applications. Asking questions is great; knowing how to find answers is even better.

Reading for Every Child: Phonics provides a flexible set of tools to support your reading program. The worksheets and activities included here may be used in many ways. Feel free to skip around or modify them to meet your needs. Family involvement is also crucial to literacy development. Communicate your lessons and goals to students' families for continuity in learning. Encourage family members to read to and with their children on a regular basis—even after the students are able to read independently.

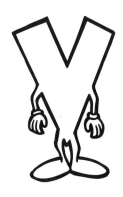

Skills Assessment

Synonyms, Consonant Blends, and Digraphs

Directions: Write the letters to complete the word that means that same as the bold word.

1. **road** = _____eet
   spr   thr   spl   str

2. **boat** = _____ip
   qu   sh   ch   fr

3. **squirt** = _____ay
   spl   str   spr   thr

4. **hold** = _____asp
   gr   th   br   cr

5. **powerful** = _____ong
   spl   str   thr   tw

6. **talk** = _____at
   ch   sc   sp   sn

7. **little** = _____all
   sm   nt   nk   sh

8. **plate** = di_____
   st   nt   nk   sh

9. **trail** = pa_____
   st   nt   th   sh

10. **penny** = ce_____
    st   nt   nk   sh

Prefixes and Suffixes

Directions: Circle the word that fits each definition.

11. **do again**	remember	redo	undo
12. **full of thanks**	thankless	thanking	thankful
13. **more happy**	happy	happier	happiest
14. **to view before**	preview	viewer	overview
15. **to not believe**	believer	disbelieve	believing
16. **without use**	useful	useable	useless

Skills Assessment (cont.)

Antonyms and Vowel Sounds

Directions: Mark the circle in front of the word that is the antonym of the bold word.

17. **women**   ○ men   ○ mane   ○ mean

18. **early**   ○ last   ○ lot   ○ late

19. **fast**   ○ sleep   ○ slow   ○ cloud

20. **cold**   ○ hot   ○ caught   ○ hold

21. **up**   ○ deer   ○ dawn   ○ down

Contractions, Possessives, and Plurals

Directions: Underline the correct word for each sentence.

22. The (**girl**, **girl's**, **girls**) backpack was red.

23. The (**dogs**, **dog**, **dog's**) leash was on the stairs.

24. He pointed to the three (**man**, **man's**, **men**).

25. All of the (**child**, **children**, **child's**) were on the bus.

26. (**They're**, **They's**, **They'll**) coming over for dinner.

Homophones

Directions: Circle the word that sounds the same as the bold word.

27. **tail**   teal   tile   tale

28. **meet**   mate   meat   might

29. **site**   sit   sight   seat

30. **tow**   toe   two   too

Over Land and Sea

Directions: Read each sentence. Write one of the consonants from the box on each line so the word makes sense in the sentence.

m r v b h l s

1. That __m__ountain peak is high.

2. The city is next to a big ____iver.

3. The farm is down in a ____alley.

4. There is a lot of water in that ____ake.

5. I rode my bike up the ____ill.

6. There is a ship down in the ____ay.

7. The ship is safe in the ____arbor.

8. Birds fly over the ____ea.

9. A ____ook of maps is called an atlas.

10. Dad drove our ____an up the hill.

11. Farmers grow crops on their ____and.

12. We made a tower out of wet ____and.

 **Extra.**

Write a list of words that begin with each of the letters in the box.

 **Phonics**

Clue Factory

Directions: Read each word and the clue. Change the first letter to make a new word that matches the clue. Use the letters on the boxes.

Word	Clue	New Word
1. **s**ite	fly it	_k_ ite
2. **c**an	cook in it	___an
3. **v**an	cool off with this	___an
4. **h**eel	do this to a banana	___eel
5. **b**est	for bird eggs	___est
6. **b**ug	to pull	___ug
7. **b**ell	for water	___ell
8. **d**en	write with it	___en
9. **v**ote	a letter	___ote
10. **s**ings	a bird has two	___ings
11. **m**en	after nine	___en
12. **l**umber	four, five, or six	___umber
13. **c**ake	not real	___ake
14. **g**ave	on the ocean	___ave

Rhyming Riddles

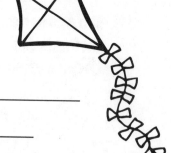

Directions: Read each riddle and the answers on the clouds. Write each answer on the line.

1. What is two thousand pounds of toys? _____

2. What do you call a row of trees? _____

3. What do you call a storm sewer? _____

4. What does a mama cricket give her baby? _____

5. Where can dogs run and play? _____

6. What do you call the highest jump? _____

7. Where can you fly on a windy day? _____

8. What do you call the king of the forest? _____

9. Where do the ducks get together? _____

10. What is another name for a goldfish? _____

Sir Fur · on Bill Hill · a rain drain · a bug hug · a bark park · a pine line · a fun ton · a wet pet · at a kite site · the top hop

 **Phonics**

A Quick Change

Directions: Read each word and the sentence. Change the word so it fits the clue. Write the new word on the line.

	Word	**Clue**
1.	made	My mom was ___*mad*___ at me.
2.	fad	Those jeans will ___*fade*___ in the wash.
3.	tap	He will _____ them together.
4.	fate	That is a _____ old cat.
5.	pan	Who broke that window _____?
6.	cap	The red _____ hung down his back.
7.	man	His horse has a long, shiny _____.
8.	cane	I _____ come over to your house.
9.	vane	We will come in the _____.
10.	rid	We will _____ in the car.
11.	fin	It was a _____ day.
12.	ripe	The jeans had a _____ at the knee.
13.	site	Come and _____ here beside me.
14.	hop	I _____ you win the race.

Rain Parade

Directions: Read the words in each raindrop. Color the raindrop with the long vowel sound.

1.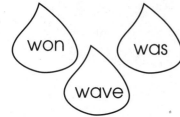
won   was   wave

6.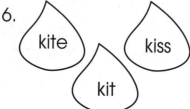
kite   kiss   kit

11.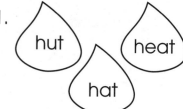
hut   heat   hat

2.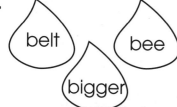
belt   bee   bigger

7.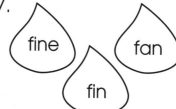
fine   fan   fin

12.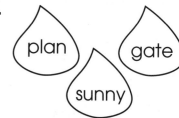
plan   gate   sunny

3.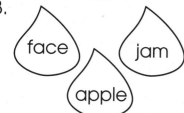
face   jam   apple

8.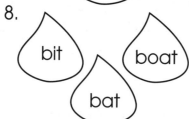
bit   boat   bat

13.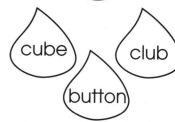
cube   club   button

4.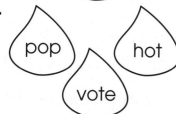
pop   hot   vote

9.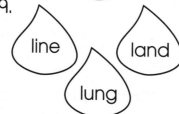
line   land   lung

14.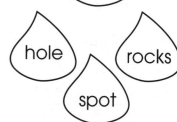
hole   rocks   spot

5.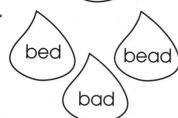
bed   bead   bad

10.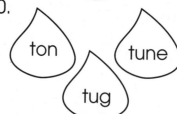
ton   tune   tug

15.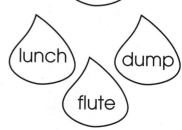
lunch   dump   flute

 Extra.

Create more raindrops for this page. Write two short-vowel words and one long-vowel word inside each raindrop. Exchange papers with a classmate.

Summer Day

Directions: Read the story. Then write each underlined word in the correct column.

Last weekend, Kim invited me over to her house. She was having a garage <u>sale</u> and needed some <u>help</u>. When I arrived, there were <u>ten</u> people <u>lined</u> up at the <u>gate</u>. Kim <u>ran</u> the register. I helped people with their <u>bags</u>.

Later, we <u>rode</u> our <u>bikes</u> down to the park. Kim's <u>little</u> brother Jake wanted to come, too. We played on the swings, while he <u>chased</u> butterflies with a <u>net</u>. Jake is <u>five</u> years old. He can be <u>cute</u> sometimes.

It was a <u>hot</u> day, so we <u>came</u> back early. We sat on the porch and drank <u>pop</u>. When the <u>sun</u> set, I had to head <u>home</u>. It was a really <u>fun</u> day.

Short-Vowel Words	**Long-Vowel Words**
_____	_____
_____	_____
_____	_____
_____	_____
_____	_____
_____	_____
_____	_____
_____	_____

 **Phonics**

Cecee's Cake

Directions: Read each word in the box. If the word begins with a **hard c**, write it under the **cake**. If the word begins with a **soft c**, write it under the **city**.

center	cake	cow	curb
circus	city	cider	cage
come	coat	cone	circle
cement	cent	cane	cell

Hard C Words

Soft C Words

_____   _____

_____   _____

_____   _____

_____   _____

_____   _____

_____   _____

_____   _____

0-7424-2833-8 *Reading for Every Child: Phonics*

 **Phonics**

Get in the Game

Directions: Circle **gym** if the bold letter has a **soft g** sound.
Circle **gate** if the bold letter has the **hard g** sound.

1. lar**g**e   gym
              gate

2. a**g**e   gym
              gate

3. wa**g**on   gym
              gate

4. **g**iant   gym
              gate

5. **g**ave   gym
              gate

6. do**g**   gym
              gate

7. pa**g**e   gym
              gate

8. **g**ame   gym
              gate

9. **g**as   gym
              gate

10. **g**erm   gym
              gate

11. hu**g**e   gym
              gate

12. **g**irl   gym
              gate

13. a**g**o   gym
              gate

14. **g**entle gym
              gate

0-7424-2833-8 *Reading for Every Child: Phonics*

The Scary Story Club

Directions: Use the key to write the missing letters in the message below.

Key

1 = sp   2 = st   3 = sc

Scary Story Club Meeting This Tuesday!

Bring a __1__ooky __3__arf and your be__2__ fake

__3__abs! The __3__ary __2__ory Club will meet at __2__eve's

house on Tuesday. __2__op by to share your __2__ories.

__1__in a tale about __3__ary __1__iders or monsters

that turn __2__udents to __2__one.

Don't be shy to __1__eak! Share your tale and

ca__2__ a __1__ell. __2__ay to hear all of the __2__ories! It

would be a shame to miss this __1__ecial meeting.

 Extra.

Use a few of the words above to write a scary story you
could share at the meeting.

Phonics

two-letter blends (br, cr, dr, fr, gr, tr)

Danger!

Directions: Read each sentence. Use the blends on the train to write in the missing letters. Then write the completed word.

1. Today was like a bad _dr_eam. ____dream____

2. The sky was ____ay and rainy. _____

3. The ____ain had to travel a long distance.

   _____

4. The ranchers needed the ____ain to feed their animals. _____

5. There was a ____ight flash in the sky. _____

6. Big ____ops of rain began to pelt down. _____

7. The engineer picked up a ____own paper bag.

   _____

8. He pulled out a thick slice of ____ead. _____

9. He gave the brakeman some ____uit. _____

10. It was going to be a long ____ip. _____

11. There was a ____ack of thunder. _____

12. The engine roared like a ____agon. _____

13. The train had to ____oss a broken bridge. _____

14. The engineer had to be very ____ave. _____

Flickering Flames

Directions: Read each sentence and the three choices.
Circle the one that makes sense in the sentence.

1. The rose started to (**blew, bloom, blanket**) in the sun.

2. The day turned (**cloudy, clock, clean**) and gray.

3. I used too much (**glove, gloom, glue**) on my card.

4. She hurt her knee on the (**slippers, slide, slow**).

5. Jupiter is the biggest (**plant, plate, planet**) in our solar system.

6. The (**flames, flower, flip**) from the fire danced for hours.

Directions: Write a sentence for each of the following words.

7. glasses _____

_____

8. clock _____

_____

9. plant _____

_____

10. blister _____

_____

 **Extra.**

Write tongue twisters for each blend (bl, gl, cl, fl, pl, sl). For example, Trevor tried to trim the tree. Share your twisters with classmates.

Spring Flowers

Directions: Read each clue. Write one of the blends from the flower box to finish each word.

spr   str   thr   spl   scr

1. front of your neck — _thr_ oat
2. puddle play — _____ ash
3. grow taller — _____ out
4. a bit of wood — _____ inter
5. an itch wants this — _____ atch
6. to crack — _____ it
7. a bug-stopper — _____ een
8. a season — _____ ing
9. sip through this — _____ aw
10. a yell — _____ eam
11. after two — _____ ee
12. powerful — _____ ong
13. for sewing — _____ ead
14. city road — _____ eet

⭐ **Extra.**

Create a list of additional words that begin with the letters in the box above. Write clues for each word and challenge a classmate to guess your words.

Summer Break

Directions: Write **nd**, **nt**, or **nk** on each line to complete the word.

1. During the summer, I like to spe_nd_ time at the lake.

2. I enjoy digging for treasures in the sa____.

3 It's fun to walk barefoot on the river ba____.

4. My brother Miguel likes to camp outside in his te____.

5. We always seem to get our pa____s really dirty.

6. When there's a good wi____, we can fly kites in the field.

7. Miguel hu____s for frogs and snakes by the water.

8. I thi____ he tries to get as dirty as possible.

9. He likes to make up crazy stu____s for us to try.

10. When it gets hot, we like to dri____ lemonade in the shade.

11. Sometimes, we even sell lemonade in our fro____ yard.

12. We're always sad to see the summer e____.

Riding the Pony Express

Directions: Read the sentences and words at the bottom of the page. Write the word that makes sense for each sentence.

1. In the ____*past*____, mail was delivered by the Pony Express.

2. Men rode horses through _____ country to hand deliver letters.

3. The riders did not stop to _____.

4. They _____ about their dangerous trips.

5. They rode their horses all across the _____.

6. These men liked the _____ and thrill of the journey.

7. They had to ride _____ to deliver the mail.

8. The men rode through the heat and the _____.

9. The moon was their _____.

10. They were always covered with trail _____.

11. Pony Express riders no longer _____ into the saddle.

12. Carrying mail is a _____ for trucks and planes.

risk	task	lamp	west
wild	jump	dust	rest
cold	fast	past	told

Phonics

On the High Seas

Directions: Color the space **red** if the vowel has the same sound as the **a** in **gate**.

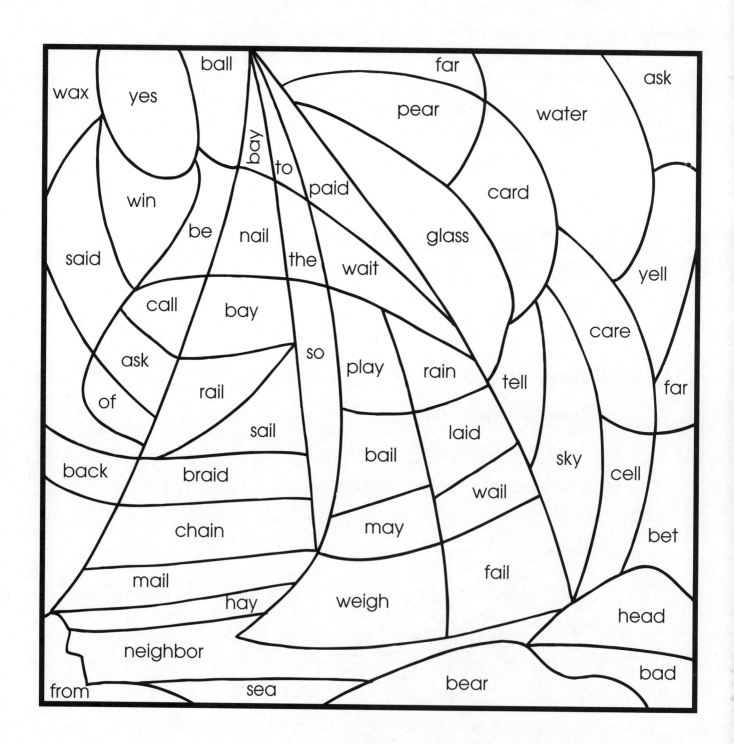

   vowel digraphs (ee, ea)

Cheer for the Team

Directions: Write the words from the banner under the correct vowel digraph.

team   real   leave
feel   east   seen   teeth
teach   free   meal   heat
                        mean

ea   **ee**

_____   _____   _____
_____   _____   _____
_____   _____   _____
_____   _____   _____

Directions: Write a sentence using the given pair of words.

1. mean, teeth _____

   _____

2. seen, leave _____

   _____

3. feel, teach _____

   _____

4. team, free _____

   _____

 Extra.

Write a team cheer using words with the **ee** and **ea** digraphs.

The "O" Team

Directions: Find the **long o** words in the puzzle. Start at any letter. Then move in any direction to the other letters until you spell a **long o** word. Write the **long o** word under the correct letter group.

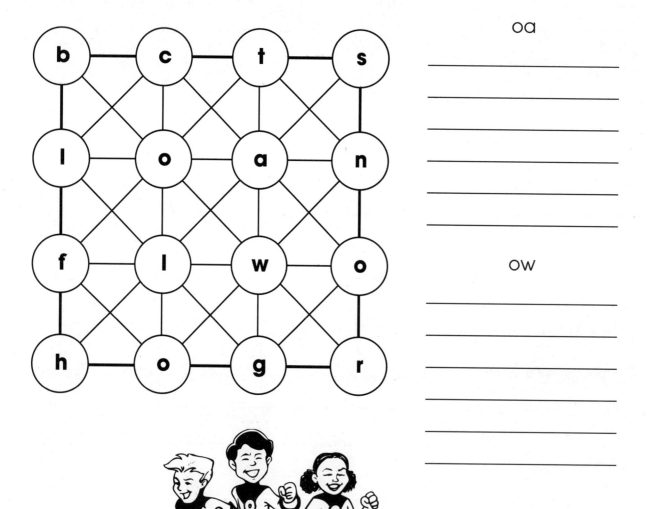

oa

_____

_____

_____

_____

_____

ow

_____

_____

_____

_____

_____

 Extra.

There are several more hidden **ow** words in the puzzle. Can you find them?

Autumn Leaves

Directions: Read each sentence and the vowel choices.
Write the correct vowel pair on the line. Then color in
that leaf.

1. I told her it wasn't my f_au_lt.   au   oo   ew

2. The m____n and stars were shining.   au   oo   ew

3. He was the n____ kid in class.   au   oo   ew

4. My plant gr____ three inches.   au   oo   ew

5. We watched the rocket l____nch.   au   oo   ew

6. What was the c____se of the accident?   au   oo   ew

7. The r____ster woke us up very early.   au   oo   ew

8. They walk to sch____l together.   au   oo   ew

9. The ball fl____ through the air.   au   oo   ew

10. I would love a sc____p of ice cream.   au   oo   ew

11. She puts meat in her s____ce.   au   oo   ew

12. His d____ghter is in my class.   au   oo   ew

13. I only had a f____ problems left to do.   au   oo   ew

14. He dropped his sp____n on the floor.   au   oo   ew

0-7424-2833-8 *Reading for Every Child: Phonics*

Crawling Along

Directions: Read each clue. Write **aw**, **ou**, or **ow** on each line to complete the word.

1. A baby does this before walking.   cr_aw_l

2. This is a sad or angry face.   fr____n

3. This is a rule not to be broken.   l____

4. This is found in the sky.   cl____d

5. You find this at a concert.   cr____d

6. It comes every morning.   d____n

7. This is the opposite of quiet.   l____d

8. Don't do this in a library.   sh____t

9. In the summer, this is mowed.   l____n

10. He makes you giggle.   cl____n

11. This is a bird's toenail.   cl____

12. You do this when you're sleepy.   y____n

13. The opposite of lost is this.   f____nd

14. You can drink milk through this.   str____

0-7424-2833-8 *Reading for Every Child: Phonics*

 **Phonics**   vowel digraphs (ie)

An Eye on the Pie

Directions: Circle the word that best completes each sentence.

1. This plant will (**day**, **down**, **die**) without water.

2. That paper plane (**flies**, **flees**, **flows**) very well.

3. The (**thaw**, **thief**, **throat**) stole our money.

4. He wore a blue (**tea**, **tow**, **tie**) with his suit.

5. The knight had a silver (**shield**, **show**, **shoulder**).

6. I didn't tell a (**lay**, **low**, **lie**).

7. There is a cow in that (**failed**, **field**, **fouled**).

8. The man in the suit is the (**chief**, **chow**, **choose**).

Directions: Look at each circled word above. Write the word under the **pie** if **ie** has the long **i** sound. Write the word under the **shield** if **ie** has the long **e** sound.

_____   _____

_____   _____

_____   _____

27

The Pony and the Fly

Directions: Read the words on the pony. Decide what sound the **y** makes in each one. Write the words in the correct columns below.

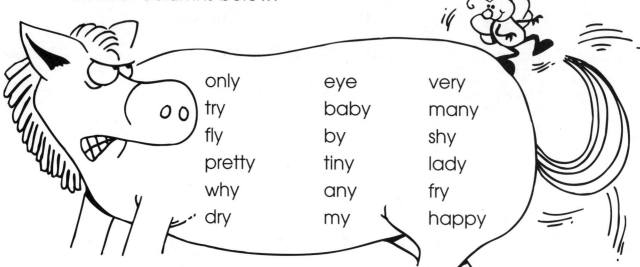

only	eye	very
try	baby	many
fly	by	shy
pretty	tiny	lady
why	any	fry
dry	my	happy

y sounds like i   **y sounds like e**

_____   _____

_____   _____

_____   _____

_____   _____

_____   _____

_____   _____

_____   _____

 Extra.

Use several words from this page to write a short story about the pony and the fly.

 **Phonics**

Two Sounds of OO

Directions: Read each word. Color the space **blue** if the word has the same vowel sound as in **moon**. Color the space **yellow** if the word has the same vowel sound as in **wood**.

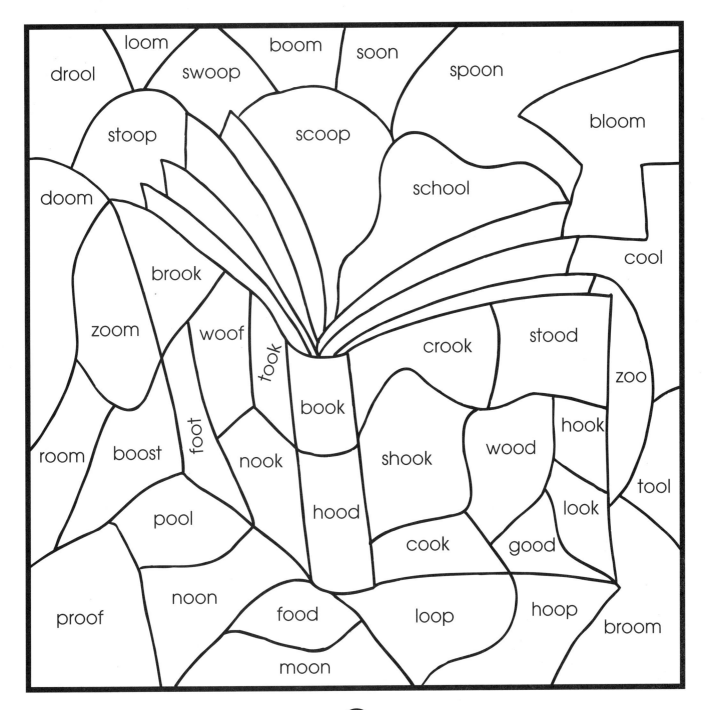

Phonics   consonant digraphs (sh, ch)

Message in a Bottle

Directions: Write **sh** or **ch** on each line to complete the message.

Dear Friend,

This is my last ___ance. It is a ___ame I ___all never
see the treasure ___est and all its gold. But be of good
___eer. Your luck is about to ___ange.

In this bottle is a ___art that will ___ow you the way
to our sunken ___ip. Once it sailed proudly on the sea, but
now it is down on the bottom with the ___ells. The ___est
is in the captain's room. A big ___ain is around it. The
___ain is closed with a lock. The key is here for you.
___ake the bottle and it ___ould come out.

Look ___arp and keep your mouth ___ut or your time
as a ri___ man will be ___ort. It makes me happy to
___are this with you and your ___ildren. Others in the
crew may still be alive. They might ___ase you if they find
out you have the gold, but keep your ___in up. I know
you will win in the end.

Sir Shadrach,
the Pirate

Phonics

Our Field Trip

Directions: Mark the circle in front of the word that completes each sentence.

SS WHALE

1. Our _____ grade class took a trip.
   ○ thing   ● third   ○ think

2. At first, I didn't _____ it would be fun.
   ○ thing   ○ third   ○ think

3. We were going to see _____.
   ○ whales   ○ wheels   ○ whole

4. I was sure we wouldn't see _____.
   ○ than   ○ the   ○ them

5. A storm blew in _____ we were on the boat.
   ○ which   ○ while   ○ white

6. _____ rolled across the sky.
   ○ Thunder   ○ There   ○ Though

7. The waves seemed higher _____ mountains.
   ○ this   ○ than   ○ them

8. _____ the storm was over.
   ○ Then   ○ Than   ○ Them

9. I saw the first _____.
   ○ which   ○ white   ○ whale

10. _____ were two more.
    ○ Throat   ○ Thing   ○ There

0-7424-2833-8 *Reading for Every Child: Phonics*

Our Field Trip (cont.)

11. I don't know _____, but they liked the boat.
   ○ while   ○ why   ○ wheat

12. We saw _____ more.
   ○ three   ○ which   ○ then

13. We did not _____ anything into the water.
   ○ three   ○ throw   ○ through

14. _____ all glided away.
   ○ Threw   ○ Throat   ○ They

15. _____ did they go?
   ○ Though   ○ There   ○ Where

16. _____ was the best part of the trip.
   ○ That   ○ Whip   ○ The

17. I wanted to _____ the man who showed us the whales.
   ○ which   ○ threw   ○ thank

18. He knew just _____ to say.
   ○ what   ○ these   ○ whip

19. _____ trip was great.
   ○ When   ○ Through   ○ The

 **Phonics**

Space Safari

Directions: Use the letters on the planets to finish the words in the sentences below. Then write the new word.

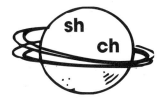 

1. The space _sh_ ip is ready for take off.

   ___spaceship___

2. The astronauts ____ook hands with the President of the United States before they boarded.

   _____

3. ____ills ran up and down the astronauts' spines as the countdown began. _____

4. People were pu____ing buttons as the countdown continued. _____

5. "____at a beautiful site!" one astronaut later cried as she saw Earth. _____

6. The astronauts kept checking their ____arts as they flew. _____

7. These brave people had ____osen a difficult but exciting job. _____

8. When they spla____ed down two weeks later, they would have many things to report. _____

33

0-7424-2833-8 *Reading for Every Child: Phonics*

More Rhyming Riddles

Directions: Read the riddles and the answers along the king's robe. Write the answer to each riddle on the line.

1. What do you call it when the sound from a bell keeps echoing? _____*long gong*_____

2. What do you call loud singing? _____

3. What do you find on a royal finger? _____

4. What do you call bug bite you get at the playground?

   _____

5. What do you call it when you practice your times tables as you wash up at night? _____

6. What do giant rodents use to make their pants? _____

7. What special tooth does a bell monster have? _____

8. What is another name for a wasp? _____

9. What do you call washing after a hike? _____

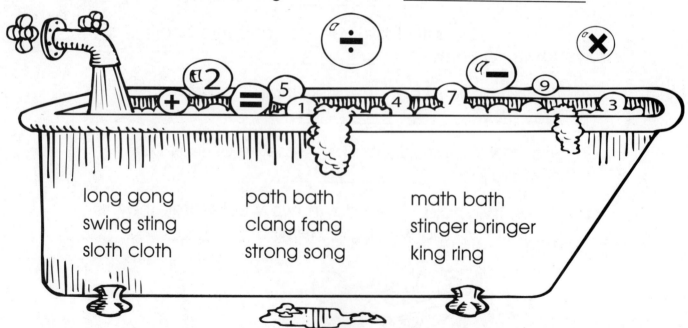

long gong	path bath	math bath
swing sting	clang fang	stinger bringer
sloth cloth	strong song	king ring

Phonics

The Laughing Elephant

Directions: Read each sentence and the words in the bank. Write the word on the line that makes sense in the sentence. Then find the word in the puzzle.

1. The baby _____ didn't wander far from its mother.

2. She sang the _____ to Grandma over the _____.

3. The meat cooked too long and was very _____.

4. Dad keeps a _____ of me in his wallet.

5. He didn't get _____ sleep due to his _____.

6. You'll _____ when you read this story.

7. The road was _____ after the storm.

8. I babysat my _____ last weekend.

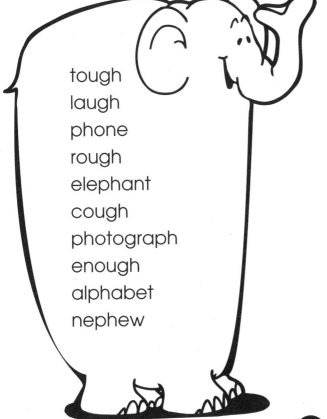

tough
laugh
phone
rough
elephant
cough
photograph
enough
alphabet
nephew

T	T	H	C	P	B	C	M
E	O	G	R	H	L	G	H
B	U	U	Y	O	B	G	L
A	G	O	X	T	U	A	O
H	H	C	B	O	U	G	P
P	Q	K	N	G	N	A	H
L	N	E	H	R	S	P	O
A	E	T	Y	A	W	F	N
T	N	A	H	P	E	L	E
O	N	E	P	H	E	W	E

A Whale of a Puzzle

Directions: Read each sentence clue and the words in the bank. Write the missing words in the puzzle.

Across

3. The dog didn't _____ me.

5. I saw _____ over there.

6. The clerk gave me the _____.

8. I had a cold and a bad _____.

11. I will _____ you how to do it.

14. I like to _____ baseball games.

15. _____ were three of them.

16. Aladdin had _____ wishes.

17. The ground was _____.

Down

1. The bells started to _____.

2. I know _____ he is.

3. We ate dip and _____.

4. I learned to read in _____.

5. The meat was _____.

7. She had _____ money to buy the ticket.

9. My _____ drove us there.

10. Snow is cold and _____.

11. Put a clean _____ on the bed.

12. I want the _____ one.

13. The joke made me _____.

14. _____ did you do?

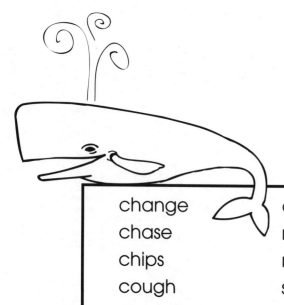

change	other	there
chase	ring	three
chips	rough	tough
cough	school	watch
enough	sheet	what
father	show	where
laugh	them	white

 **Phonics**

A Whale of a Puzzle (cont.)

0-7424-2833-8 *Reading for Every Child: Phonics*

Starry, Starry Night

Directions: Unscramble each word. Write it on the line to complete the sentence.

1. jra   There is still some jam in the ____*jar*____.

2. rta   They use _____ to patch the road.

3. sart   I wish on the first _____ I see.

4. rcsa   That burn will leave a _____.

5. drha   This is a very _____ trick.

6. dyar   We have a pine tree in our _____.

7. rbka   Did you hear my dog _____?

8. arc   We have a new _____.

9. pkar   We will eat in the _____.

10. kmar   I will _____ the trail so we won't get lost.

11. rdak   It is _____ at night.

12. tpra   This is my favorite _____ of the movie!

13. akrhs   The _____ glided through the water.

Phonics

Lucky Clover

Directions: Look at each clover. Fill in the blank with **er, ir, or,** or **ur** to complete each word.

1. p_**ur**_ple

2. b____d

3. h____n

4. slipp____

5. n____se

6. st____m

7. th____ty

8. t____key

9. f____n

Directions: Read the sentences and the word choices. Circle the word that makes sense in each sentence.

10. I go shopping every Saturday (**morning, market**).

11. She used a broom to sweep the front (**perch, porch**).

12. We were lucky the storm did not (**hurt, hunt**) anyone.

13. He wore his new (**shot, shirt**) to school today.

14. They took a wrong (**turn, tune**) and got lost.

 Extra.

Try to write one sentence using at least two r-controlled vowel sounds.

Roy's Coins

Directions: Read the paragraphs. Circle all of the words that contain the vowel sound you hear in the word **oil**.

Roy wants to join the Coin Club at school. Some of the boys in his class are in the club. They enjoy finding new coins. They say coins are more fun than most toys. Nothing matches the joy of finding a coin nobody else has.

They clean their coins with stiff brushes and soft, moist rags. They toil long and hard to get rid of the tarnish and soil. One boy tried to boil an old Roman coin, but it didn't help. He still had to scrub the dirt off.

The members of the club point out their best coins to their friends. Roy's father gave him some candy coins to share. They are wrapped in gold foil. Roy wants to avoid showing them to anyone before the meeting. He doesn't want to spoil the surprise.

Directions: Find and write twelve **oi** or **oy** words from the selection.

_____   _____

_____   _____

_____   _____

_____   _____

_____   _____

_____   _____

Special Vowels

Directions: Read the clues and the list of words.
Write the word from the list that matches each clue.

1. something that helps keep
   machines running   _____

2. loud sounds together   _____

3. to yell   _____

4. a night bird   _____

5. a farm tool that loosens dirt   _____

6. things that children play with   _____

7. a group of many people   _____

8. to hit with a hammer   _____

9. something that water does
   when it gets very hot   _____

10. another name for dirt   _____

11. the sharp end of something   _____

12. the part of the face used to smile   _____

13. a very tall building   _____

14. a young man   _____

pound	tower	noise	toys	mouth
oil	plow	point	boils	owl
shout	soil	boy	crowd	

Knock Knock

Directions: Circle the word that starts with the same sound as the bold word.

1. **wrote**	won	ripe	open
2. **knee**	nice	key	eat
3. **wrist**	in	will	run
4. **knock**	code	October	note
5. **knight**	king	never	go
6. **write**	real	white	won't
7. **wrong**	rake	well	on
8. **knew**	clue	cow	nest
9. **knife**	cute	next	kite
10. **kneel**	eat	cape	nap
11. **wrap**	ran	apple	win
12. **know**	cab	ouch	net
13. **knob**	cob	needle	key

⭐ **Extra.**

Can you think of any more words that begin with **wr** or **kn**? Write a list for each on a separate piece of paper.

A Brave Knight

Directions: Read the story below. Use the words from the Word Bank to fill in the blanks. Circle the silent letters in each of the words that you write.

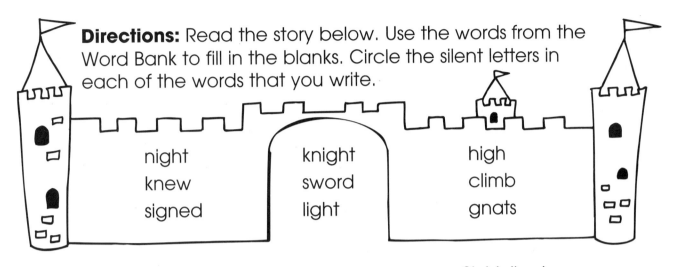

night	knight	high
knew	sword	climb
signed	light	gnats

It was a dark and stormy _____. Sir Valiant, a _____ of King Machai's court, had just finished reading a letter. Even though the letter was not _____, he _____ that it was from the beautiful Princess Kaylee. The letter begged him to rescue her from the tower of Bigbad Castle.

Sir Valiant knew the castle was _____ in the mountains. It was surrounded by many trees that blocked out the _____ of the sun. He also heard about the clouds of pesky _____ that flew around your head if you dared to go into the woods.

He took a deep breath. He knew that a true knight would be brave. He decided to _____ the mountain and find the princess. The knight picked up his _____, jumped on his horse, and headed toward the woods.

 Extra.

Write an ending to this story. Try to use words with silent letters in your story. Underline those words.

Summer Camp

Directions: Read the story. Circle the words that have a silent consonant. Write those words on the tent below.

Keoni and Hector were ready. They would be leaving soon. The two boys were going to summer camp. They knew about camping in the woods. They packed their pocket knife and a flashlight.

The boys wanted to have some fun. Keoni wanted to climb the rock wall. Hector liked to write stories. He wrote about his hikes in the woods. Neither of them liked the pesky gnats near the water.

Last summer, Hector won the water fight but hurt his wrist. He had to wear a wrap for a few days. Keoni taught some other boys how to fish. They caught enough fish to feed everyone at camp!

 Extra.

Write a story about a camp or sleepover experience. After writing it, underline any words that have silent consonants in them. Share your story with classmates.

 **Phonics**

Chasing Jojo

Directions: Add **ed** and **ing** to each word to make two new words. Write them on the lines.

1.	walk	walked	walking
2.	enjoy	_____	_____
3.	burn	_____	_____
4.	clean	_____	_____
5.	cough	_____	_____
6.	dance	_____	_____
7.	brush	_____	_____
8.	chew	_____	_____

Directions: Add **ed** or **ing** to the word in parentheses. Write the new form on the line to complete the sentence.

9. We ___covered___ our heads when the rain started.
   (cover)

10. The dog came _____ through the gate.
    (crash)

11. I _____ that question in class.
    (ask)

12. She is _____ your mom right now.
    (call)

13. Don't add the noodles until the water is _____.
    (boil)

14. They were _____ and ready to go by noon.
    (dress)

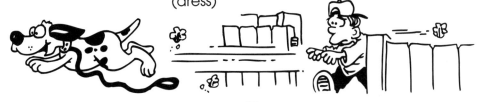

0-7424-2833-8 *Reading for Every Child: Phonics*

Tall, Taller, Tallest

Directions: Add **er** and **est** to each word to make two new words. Hint: If the word ends with **y**, change the **y** to an **i** before you add the ending.

1. happy   _happier_   _happiest_
2. strong   _____   _____
3. green   _____   _____
4. short   _____   _____
5. kind   _____   _____
6. curly   _____   _____
7. new   _____   _____
8. tough   _____   _____
9. quick   _____   _____
10. old   _____   _____

Directions: Read the sentence. Look at the word in parentheses. Write the correct form of the word in parentheses on the line.

11. This is the _____ pie I've ever eaten!
(great)

12. He jumped a foot _____ than his brother.
(long)

13. I was the _____ runner in the class.
(fast)

14. It was _____ before my sister started crying.
(quiet)

⭐ **Extra.**

Use the *Guinness Book of World Records* to find the tallest, oldest, and strangest animals, places, and things. Share your findings with your classmates.

Helpful Suffixes

Directions: Add **ful** and **less** to the end of each base word to make two new words.

1.	color	*colorful*	*colorless*
2.	hope	_____	_____
3.	power	_____	_____
4.	thought	_____	_____
5.	use	_____	_____
6.	care	_____	_____
7.	help	_____	_____
8.	harm	_____	_____
9.	thank	_____	_____
10.	fear	_____	_____

Directions: Read each sentence. Write one of the words you created above to finish each thought.

11. The _____ flags were red, yellow, and green.

12. His pet snake had no poison, so it was _____.

13. She was _____ that she had the winning ticket.

14. He hadn't studied so he was _____ of getting a bad grade.

15. The great new video game was a _____ gift from his aunt.

Artful Endings

Directions: Read the sentences and the list of words. Add a **y** to one of the words to complete each sentence. Write the new word on the line.

frost
cloud
stick
luck
squeak

1. We were _____ to get tickets to the concert.
2. The glue made my desk _____.
3. It was a gray and _____ day.
4. My new boots make a _____ sound.
5. When it's cold outside, our windows look _____.

Directions: Read the sentences and the list of words. Add an **ly** to one of the words to complete each sentence. Write the new word on the line.

6. He walked _____ and missed the bus.
7. She ran _____ to the crying child.
8. My dad reads a _____ newspaper.
9. She talked so _____ we could hardly hear her.
10. Our class is filled with _____ people.

soft
week
quick
friend
slow

Directions: Read each sentence. Circle the choice that has the correct suffix attached.

11. Please speak (**loudly, loudful**) when you give your speech.

12. The skunk left a (**stinkly, stinky**) smell behind.

13. He was feeling (**sleepy, sleeper**) after his long day.

14. We walk down the hallway (**quiety, quietly**).

15. I had a (**real, really**) nice time at your house.

 **Phonics**

Bookish Benita

Directions: Circle the word that completes each sentence. Write the word on the line.

1. The man was ___*childish*___ when he lost his temper.
   doable   childish   reddish

2. The sweet kitten was _____.
   puppyish   boyish   lovable

3. The job was hard but _____.
   doable   puppyish   sheepish

4. The dawn sky was _____.
   clownish   reddish   girlish

5. A girl who is always reading is _____.
   bookish   yellowish   boyish

6. Though he was old, the man had a _____ laugh.
   tall   doable   boyish

7. In early spring, the hills have a _____ tint.
   babyish   bookish   greenish

8. Another word for fun is _____.
   girlish   enjoyable   babyish

9. If a boy is _____, other boys like him.
   likeable   sheepish   greenish

10. The broken game wasn't _____.
    babyish   playable   bookish

Review and Recite

Directions: Write the base word on the line to complete each meaning.

1. **Redo** means to _____*do*_____ again.

2. **Unpaid** means not _____.

3. **Undone** means not _____.

4. **Recall** means to _____ again.

5. **Unhappy** means not _____.

6. **Unmade** means not _____.

7. **Rewrite** means to _____ again.

8. **Unable** means not _____.

Now try writing the entire meaning.

9. **Unheated** _____ *means not heated* _____.

10. **Rearrange** _____.

11. **Remake** _____.

12. **Uncooked** _____.

13. **Untied** _____.

14. **Rerun** _____.

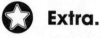 **Extra.**

Choose four words from this page to write in sentences. Or, create a poem or story using some of these words. Circle the words you use. Share your work with your classmates.

 **Phonics**

Tonight's Preview

Directions: Circle the prefix that completes each sentence. Then write it on the line.

1. We will __*pre*__ pay our phone bill.

   (pre)
   dis

2. The spot on the rug will _____ appear.

   pre
   dis

3. She will _____ heat the oven.

   pre
   dis

4. We saw the _____ view before the movie.

   pre
   dis

5. We _____ agreed about what to do next.

   pre
   dis

6. She will _____ cover something new.

   pre
   dis

7. We took a spelling _____ test.

   pre
   dis

8. It was wrong to _____ obey the rules.

   pre
   dis

9. Some people _____ like eating peas.

   pre
   dis

 Extra.

Brainstorm a list of words that begin with **pre** and **dis**. Share your lists with classmates.

Don't Oversleep!

Directions: Circle the word that matches each meaning.

1. **to do too much**	overdo	redo	undo
2. **to use too much**	reuse	underuse	overuse
3. **to treat badly**	retreat	mistreat	treatment
4. **spell wrongly**	respell	misspell	spelling
5. **to sleep too much**	oversleep	undersleep	sleeper
6. **to use wrongly or badly**	reuse	useless	misuse
7. **to understand wrongly**	misunderstand	understanding	understand
8. **to bake too long**	rebake	overbake	underbake
9. **to count wrongly**	recount	counter	miscount
10. **to hear wrongly**	overhear	mishear	hearing
11. **to pay too much**	repay	underpay	overpay
12. **to label wrongly**	relabel	mislabel	unlabel
13. **to flow over**	flow	overflow	flower
14. **named wrongly**	misnamed	renamed	unnamed
15. **to eat too much**	overeat	undereat	eater

0-7424-2833-8 *Reading for Every Child: Phonics*

Super Sleuth

Directions: Read the clues. Look at the word lists. Write the word that matches each clue on the line. Hint: the number in parentheses is the number of letters in that word.

1. the most short (8)   _____

2. more new (5)   _____

3. kind of quick (7)   _____

4. full of color (8)   _____

5. without thought (11)   _____

6. full of fear (7)   _____

7. kind of cloud (6)   _____

8. quality of a boy (6)   _____

9. quality of love (7)   _____

10. to do again (4)   _____

11. to use too much (7)   _____

12. to spell wrongly (8)   _____

13. not true (6)   _____

14. to stop appearing (9)   _____

4-letter word	**11-letter word**	**7-letter words**	**8-letter words**
redo	thoughtless	fearful	colorful
		lovable	misspell
5-letter word	**6-letter words**	overuse	shortest
newer	boyish	quickly	
	cloudy		
9-letter word	untrue		
disappear			

Super Sleuth (cont.)

Directions: Count the number of boxes for each word in the puzzle. Look in that letter list for a word that might fit. Write the word in the puzzle.

q
u
i
c
k
l
y

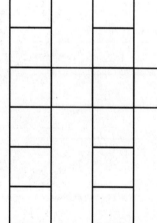

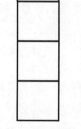

0-7424-2833-8 *Reading for Every Child: Phonics*

Birthday Surprise

Directions: Read the word on each balloon. Write the plural form of the word inside the balloon.

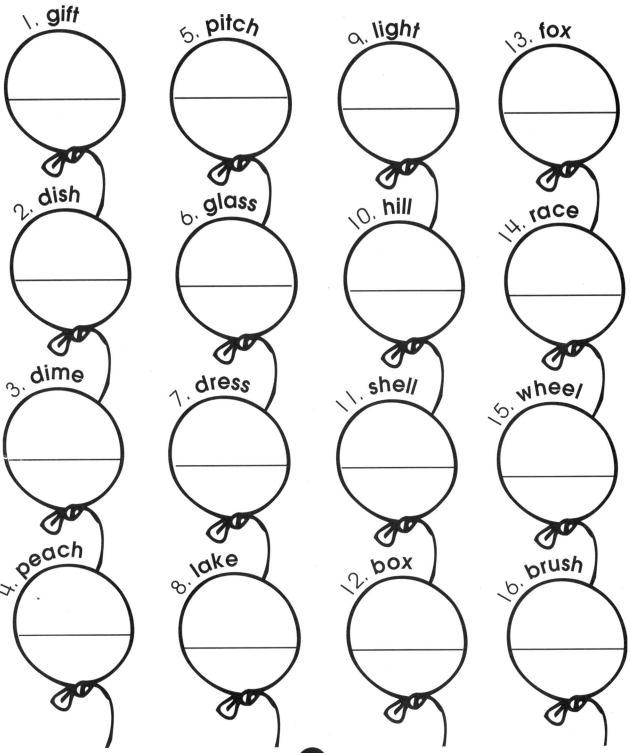

1. gift
2. dish
3. dime
4. peach
5. pitch
6. glass
7. dress
8. lake
9. light
10. hill
11. shell
12. box
13. fox
14. race
15. wheel
16. brush

Bunches of Bugs

Directions: Read each sentence. Circle the correct plural form of the word in parentheses.

1. He gathered his two (**axs, axes**) and headed into the woods.

2. She jumped over the (**benches, benchs**) to catch her dog.

3. I heard the noisy (**birdes, birds**) in the tree.

4. They carried all the (**boxes, boxs**) in from the car.

5. We milk the (**cowes, cows**) every morning.

6. Both of our (**coaches, coachs**) were at the game.

7. All of the third-grade (**classs, classes**) went on the field trip.

8. There were four (**parts, partes**) to the play.

9. My dog likes to chase the (**piges, pigs**) around the field.

10. She (**dresses, dresss**) quickly to catch the bus.

11. I enjoy riding (**horses, horses**) when I visit my aunt.

12. Have you washed the (**dishs, dishes**) yet?

13. They counted seven (**snakees, snakes**) in the garden.

14. He (**watches, watchs**) the traffic pass quickly.

 **Phonics**

Special Cases

Directions: Read each sentence. Write the plural form of a word from the list to complete each sentence.

child—children moose—moose
foot—feet goose—geese
sheep—sheep mouse—mice
tooth—teeth deer—deer
woman—women man—men

1. The _____ were tired after the long recess.

2. We need more men and _____ to volunteer.

3. I saw the three _____ by the cornfield.

4. I brush my _____ every night before I go to bed.

5. These new shoes make my _____ hurt.

6. She watched the baby _____ waddle across the street.

7. He herded the woolly _____ into the pasture.

8. During our trip to Canada, we saw _____ roaming in the open fields.

9. Many women and _____ will vote tomorrow.

10. Our cat caught three _____ outside.

Phonics

Bear's Bed

Directions: Rewrite each group of words below, adding **'s** to form words that show singular ownership.

1. the windows of a truck   _truck's windows_

2. the game that belongs to Marina   _____

3. the fur of a bear   _____

4. the bag that belongs to Chandra _____

5. the gloves that belong to the boy _____

6. the tail of the monkey   _____

Directions: Rewrite each group of words, adding an **'** or **s'** to the underlined word to show plural ownership.

7. the wings of the <u>birds</u>   _birds' wings_

8. the office used by the two <u>dentists</u> _____

9. the covers of the <u>book</u>   _____

10. the tents used by the <u>scouts</u>   _____

11. the homework done by the <u>students</u> _____

12. the field used by the <u>players</u>   _____

Phonics

The Cows' Escape

Directions: Read each sentence and the words shown below the blank. Write the correct possessive on the line.

1. The _____*dog's*_____ tail is short and curly.
   (dog's, dogs')

2. The two _____ birthdays are on the same day.
   (boy's, boys')

3. I could see the _____ heads through the window.
   (cat's, cats')

4. The _____ floors are made of wood.
   (room's, rooms')

5. Did you see _____ new puppy?
   (Mary's, Marys')

6. We took the _____ engines apart.
   (car's, cars')

7. They bought equipment for the _____ playground.
   (school's, schools')

8. The three _____ coats were on the floor.
   (girl's, girls')

9. He walked over to his _____ house.
   (neighbor's, neighbors')

10. I sat next to the _____ desk.
    (teacher's, teachers')

11. She gathered all the _____ coats.
    (guest's, guests')

12. The teacher collected the _____ papers.
    (student's, students')

compound words

An Afternoon Daydream

Directions: Write the two words that make up each compound word.

1. afternoon   <u>after</u>   <u>noon</u>
2. airplane   _____   _____
3. campfire   _____   _____
4. footstep   _____   _____
5. buttermilk   _____   _____
6. grandfather   _____   _____

Write the compound word made of the two smaller words.

7. key + board   _____
8. mountain + top   _____
9. class + room   _____
10. day + dream   _____
11. home + work   _____
12. care + free   _____
13. day + light   _____

Choose two compound words from this page. Write each one in a sentence.

14. _____

_____

15. _____

_____

 **Phonics**

Little Mountain Town

Directions: Circle the word that completes each sentence.
Write it on the line.

1. Morning sun poured into Sara's upstairs _____.

   anyone   bedroom   anything

2. She pulled on some jeans and hurried _____.

   railroad   bookcase   downstairs

3. _____ the sunlight was blinding.

   Outside   Raspberry   Sailboat

4. Sara headed down to the _____.

   scrapbook   seashore   silkworm

5. She liked to collect _____ and watch the waves.

   armload   outstanding   seashells

6. She stood on the _____ and looked up at the mountains.

   sidewalk   silkworm   grasshopper

7. This afternoon her friends would play _____ in the park.

   baseball   butterfly   snowflake

8. After sundown there would be _____.

   armload   outstanding   fireworks

9. She loved _____ about her little mountain town.

   everywhere   everything   anyone

Skill Drill

Directions: Read each contraction below. Then write the two words for which each contraction stands.

1. wouldn't   <u>would not</u>   6. he'll   _____

2. we've   _____   7. hasn't   _____

3. didn't   _____   8. she's   _____

4. that's   _____   9. won't   _____

5. we'd   _____   10. I've   _____

Directions: Read each sentence and the contractions shown below the blank. Complete the sentence by writing the two words that make up the contraction.

11. <u>They would</u> like to move to a warmer part of the country.
        (They'd)

12. He _____ like to eat right after running.
              (doesn't)

13. _____ been to the lake several times.
         (We've)

14. She _____ be able to come over tomorrow.
               (won't)

15. _____ feeling a little sick today.
          (I'm)

Name _____ Date _____

 **Phonics**

contractions

Contraction Action

Directions: Circle the contraction that completes each sentence. Then write it on the line. Don't forget to start the sentence with a capital letter.

1. _____ my dog.
(Won't, That's, She'll)

2. _____ enough for both of us.
(There's, He'll, Can't)

3. _____ ten years old.
(He's, I'll, Won't)

4. _____ come to the party.
(We'll, He's, I'm)

5. _____ show us how to do it.
(There's, They'll, She's)

6. _____ you coming?
(We'll, It's, Aren't)

7. _____ the next thing on the list?
(I'll, What's, Can't)

8. She _____ help me.
(won't, that's, she'll)

9. I _____ find it.
(there's, he'll, can't)

10. _____ up to bat first.
(We'll, He's, Can't)

11. Those boys _____ in our class.
(there's, aren't, shouldn't)

12. I _____ do that by myself.
(we'll, it's, can't)

13. You _____ home when I called.
(weren't, here's, they'll)

14. _____ be the first in line.
(Aren't, You'll, Can't)

Published by Instructional Fair. Copyright protected. 63 0-7424-2833-8 *Reading for Every Child: Phonics*

Take Note

Directions: Read the list of words and sentences. Write the word from the list that makes sense in each sentence. Draw a line between the syllables of the written word.

NOTE
A word that has a prefix or suffix can be divided into syllables between the prefix or suffix and the base word.

1. I had to ___re/write___ my story.

2. We had to _____ the gas tank before we headed home.

3. He worked hard to _____ the knot.

4. She talked so _____ we could barely hear her.

5. Before we started the lesson, we took a _____.

6. Bringing me flowers was a _____ thing to do.

7. They had a _____ night with the new baby.

8. They _____ eating vegetables.

9. On _____ days, I like to curl up with a good book.

10. The plates were _____ placed on the table.

11. Did you _____ me on the phone?

12. He ran _____ than he ever had before.

overhear
untie
pretest
sleepless
thoughtful
refill
dislike
neatly
softly
rewrite
rainy
faster

Look It Up

Directions: Read the word and divide it into syllables. Circle the one that is divided correctly. Use a dictionary to check your answers.

1.	**fever**	fe/ver	fev/er	feve/r
2.	**baby**	bab/y	ba/by	b/aby
3.	**secret**	se/cret	sec/ret	secr/et
4.	**zebra**	zebr/a	zeb/ra	ze/bra
5.	**label**	lab/el	la/bel	labe/l
6.	**spider**	spi/der	spid/er	sp/ider
7.	**tiny**	tin/y	t/iny	ti/ny
8.	**silent**	sil/ent	si/lent	sile/nt
9.	**music**	mus/ic	mu/sic	musi/c
10.	**cartoon**	car/toon	cart/oon	ca/rtoon
11.	**thirteen**	thi/rteen	thirt/een	thir/teen
12.	**garden**	ga/rden	gard/en	gar/den
13.	**umpire**	um/pire	ump/ire	u/mpire
14.	**window**	wind/ow	wi/ndow	win/dow
15.	**number**	nu/mber	num/ber	numb/er

 **Phonics**

Separating Syllables

Directions: Mark the circle in front of the choice that is divided into syllables correctly.

1. **batter**
   - ○ batt/er
   - ○ ba/tter
   - ○ bat/ter

2. **buddy**
   - ○ bud/dy
   - ○ bu/ddy
   - ○ budd/y

3. **umpire**
   - ○ ump/ire
   - ○ um/pire
   - ○ u/mpire

4. **secret**
   - ○ se/cret
   - ○ sec/ret
   - ○ secr/et

5. **undo**
   - ○ un/do
   - ○ u/ndo
   - ○ und/o

6. **tiny**
   - ○ tin/y
   - ○ ti/ny
   - ○ t/iny

7. **nothing**
   - ○ noth/ing
   - ○ not/hing
   - ○ no/thing

8. **silent**
   - ○ sil/ent
   - ○ si/lent
   - ○ silen/t

9. **spider**
   - ○ spid/er
   - ○ spide/r
   - ○ spi/der

10. **misplace**
    - ○ misp/lace
    - ○ mis/place
    - ○ mi/splace

11. **arrow**
    - ○ ar/row
    - ○ a/rrow
    - ○ arr/ow

12. **preview**
    - ○ prev/iew
    - ○ pre/view
    - ○ previ/ew

13. **mailbox**
    - ○ mai/lbox
    - ○ mailb/ox
    - ○ mail/box

14. **thirteen**
    - ○ thi/rteen
    - ○ thir/teen
    - ○ thirt/een

15. **title**
    - ○ tit/le
    - ○ ti/tle
    - ○ tit/le

16. **later**
    - ○ la/ter
    - ○ lat/er
    - ○ late/r

17. **tiptoe**
    - ○ tipt/oe
    - ○ ti/ptoe
    - ○ tip/toe

18. **zebra**
    - ○ zeb/ra
    - ○ zebr/a
    - ○ ze/bra

Synonym Means the Same

Directions: Read each analogy and the words on the banner. Write one of the choices on the line to finish the analogy.

1. Peaceful is to calm as quiet is to _____silent_____.

2. Faraway is to distant as exit is to _____.

3. Truthful is to honest as job is to _____.

4. Disappear is to vanish as tremble is to _____.

5. Hit is to strike as peek is to _____.

6. Toss is to throw as grin is to _____.

7. Smart is to clever as forest is to _____.

8. Bunny is to rabbit as puppy is to _____.

9. Fix is to repair as autumn is to _____.

10. Bucket is to pail as cheerful is to _____.

11. Find is to discover as start is to _____.

12. Unusual is to rare as beautiful is to _____.

13. Noisy is to loud as quick is to _____.

14. Angry is to mad as dirty is to _____.

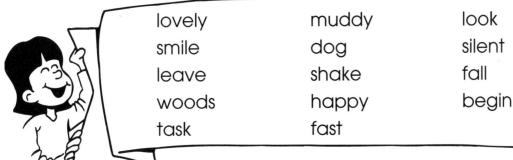

lovely	muddy	look
smile	dog	silent
leave	shake	fall
woods	happy	begin
task	fast	

Antonym Is the Opposite

Directions: Read each analogy and the answer choices. Circle the correct antonym to complete the analogy.

1. Honest is to dishonest as fast is to (**past, slow, quick**).

2. Clean is to dirty as easy is to (**early, fresh, hard**).

3. Rough is to smooth as heavy is to (**light, weighty, hearty**).

4. Dark is to light as night is to (**evening, day, dusk**).

5. Helpful is to helpless as up is to (**high, down, stairs**).

6. In is to out as under is to (**below, wonder, over**).

7. Man is to woman as boy is to (**joy, girl, son**).

8. Good is to bad as love is to (**like, hate, dove**).

9. Sunrise is to sunset as morning is to (**evening, warning, dawn**).

10. Win is to lose as dry is to (**wet, sigh, smooth**).

11. Old is to young as big is to (**huge, bug, little**).

12. New is to old as stale is to (**fresh, old, pail**).

13. Warm is to cool as hot is to (**warm, heat, cold**).

A Pair of Pears

Directions: Match the words that sound the same. Write the word from the pear next to its homophone.

1. ant _____ *aunt* _____

2. be _____

3. bare _____

4. beat _____

5. blue _____

6. breaks _____

7. by _____

8. cell _____

9. knew _____

10. knot _____

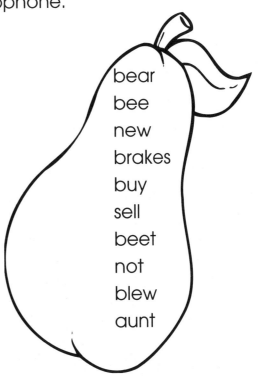

bear
bee
new
brakes
buy
sell
beet
not
blew
aunt

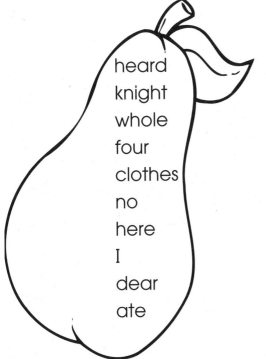

heard
knight
whole
four
clothes
no
here
I
dear
ate

11. close _____

12. deer _____

13. eight _____

14. eye _____

15. for _____

16. hear _____

17. herd _____

18. hole _____

19. know _____

20. night _____

 Extra.

Write a sentence that has a pair of homophones in it.

The Bare Bear

Directions: Circle the correct word for each sentence.

1. He (**knew**, **new**) how to spell the word.

2. She did (**knot**, **not**) lose her book this time.

3. He had (**know**, **no**) idea where his brother was.

4. The (**knight**, **night**) fought bravely.

5. She was the only (**one**, **won**) home.

6. There was only an (**our**, **hour**) of sunlight left in the day.

7. I have a new (**pear**, **pair**) of shoes.

Directions: Write the correct word for each sentence.

8. He ate a whole _____ of pie.   piece   peace

9. I want to _____ a good story.   right   write

10. She _____ a horse at the ranch.   rode   road

11. I _____ the letter.   sent   scent

12. _____ are only two books.   Their   There

13. I hurt my _____ last night.   toe   tow

14. Please _____ for me.   wait   weight

15. My _____ sent me a gift.   ant   aunt

Same but Different

Directions: Circle the word that rhymes with the boldface
word in each sentence.

1. I will **read** that book next week.
   feed   fed

2. **Lead** is very heavy.
   feed   fed

3. **Does** your mom know?
   fuzz   clothes

4. How long does a fly **live**?
   hive   give

5. The **cow** moved slowly.
   how   know

6. I sit in the first **row** in class.
   cow   know

7. The nurse fixed his **wound**.
   tuned   found

8. She will **lead** the way.
   said   bead

9. He **read** that book last week.
   bed   seed

10. We were on **live** television.
    hive   give

11. I **wound** the yarn into a ball.
    tuned   found

12. I know how to tie a **bow**.
    cow   know

13. He will **tear** up that paper.
    hear   bear

14. We took a **bow** after we sang.
    cow   know

15. A **tear** came to her eye.
    hear   bear

16. I saw two **does** in the field.
    glows   buzz

Brain Busters

Directions: Choose the word that completes each analogy. Write it on the line. Some pairs are synonyms, some are antonyms, and some are homophones. Read carefully.

1. Wait is to weight as tale is to _____.
   truth   sail   tail

2. Spend is to save as take is to _____.
   give   make   grab

3. Yes is to no as always is to _____.
   ways   never   forever

4. Knew is to new as sale is to _____.
   cheap   sail   penny

5. Present is to gift as close is to _____.
   far   clear   near

6. Hurry is to rush as hurt is to _____.
   heal   harm   dirt

7. Bought is to sold as happy is to _____.
   joyful   sad   happen

8. Week is to weak as your is to _____.
   my   his   you're

9. Trail is to path as tale is to _____.
   story   fail   bath

10. Sink is to float as whisper is to _____.
    shout   while   scissors

Write the Order

Directions: Write each set of words in alphabetical order.

1. does   _____
   fire   _____
   clothes   _____
   around   _____
   eight   _____
   buy   _____

3. round   _____
   second   _____
   night   _____
   mouth   _____
   pair   _____
   quick   _____

2. itself   _____
   keep   _____
   just   _____
   give   _____
   lamb   _____
   head   _____

4. woman   _____
   zipper   _____
   very   _____
   though   _____
   until   _____
   yellow   _____

Ready, Set, March!

Directions: Circle the word that comes first in alphabetical order.

1. blue
   back
   bring

2. pond
   play
   pen

3. scream
   strange
   skunk

4. free
   fair
   fun

5. coin
   coin
   car

6. king
   koala
   knight

7. scene
   shape
   save

8. wet
   with
   what

9. dim
   draw
   day

10. coast
    cast
    close

Directions: Write each set of words in alphabetical order.

11. soft, sand, send _____

12. gum, gave, germ _____

13. ram, ride, rode _____

14. mask, must, most _____

15. bedding, black, batter _____

Putting It Together

Directions: Mark the circle in front of the sentence that tells about the picture.

1.
   - ○ The book was in the closet.
   - ○ The book was on the top shelf.
   - ○ The boy wanted his lunch.

2.
   - ○ They sailed a boat around the lake.
   - ○ They ate lunch in the park.
   - ○ They painted pictures of a sailboat.

3.
   - ○ She left her bike out in the rain.
   - ○ She gave her bike to a friend.
   - ○ She put her bike away carefully.

4.
   - ○ He walked on the beach.
   - ○ He bought new shoes.
   - ○ He went to his friend's house.

5.
   - ○ They ate dinner at home.
   - ○ They had a picnic in the park.
   - ○ They played on the swings at the park.

6.
   - ○ The princess sang at the ball.
   - ○ The princess told a beautiful story.
   - ○ The princess danced with the prince.

Matching Meanings

Directions: Read the sentences. Write the letter of the sentence in the second group that has the same meaning on the line.

1. ___ I have to rewrite my story.
2. ___ I had a sleepless night.
3. ___ There was a snowstorm yesterday.
4. ___ Raindrops pounded on the roof.
5. ___ The old porch was unsafe.
6. ___ We had to replace the lightbulb.
7. ___ My new shirt isn't washable.
8. ___ The toys were reachable.
9. ___ The sky was filled with clouds.
10. ___ The dog was harmless.
11. ___ We have to write a weekly report.
12. ___ Our game tickets were prepaid.

A. I can't wash my new shirt.
B. The porch wasn't safe.
C. We changed the lightbulb.
D. I was awake all night.
E. Yesterday was a snowy day.
F. I have to write my story again.
G. It rained hard.
H. We write a report every week.
I. It was cloudy outside.
J. The dog wouldn't bite.
K. We paid for our tickets before the game.
L. We could reach the toys.

Answer Key

Skills Assessment ....page 6
1. str
2. sh
3. spr
4. gr
5. str
6. ch
7. sm
8. sh
9. th
10. nt
11. redo
12. thankful
13. happier
14. preview
15. disbelieve
16. useless
17. men
18. late
19. slow
20. hot
21. down
22. girl's
23. dog's
24. men
25. children
26. They're
27. tale
28. meat
29. sight
30. toe

Over Land and Sea.......page 8
1. m   5. h   9. b
2. r   6. b   10. v
3. v   7. h   11. l
4. l   8. s   12. s

Clue Factory ....page 9
1. k   6. t   11. t
2. p   7. w   12. n
3. f   8. p   13. f
4. p   9. n   14. w
5. n   10. w

Rhyming Riddles ....page 10
1. a fun ton
2. a pine line
3. a rain drain
4. a bug hug
5. a bark park
6. the top hop
7. at a kite site
8. Sir Fur
9. on Bill Hill
10. a wet pet

A Quick Change ....page 11
1. mad   8. can
2. fade   9. van
3. tape   10. ride
4. fat   11. fine
5. pane   12. rip
6. cape   13. sit
7. mane   14. hope

Rain Parade ....page 12
1. wave   9. line
2. bee   10. tune
3. face   11. heat
4. vote   12. gate
5. bead   13. cube
6. kite   14. hole
7. fine   15. flute
8. boat

Summer Day................page 13
short-vowel words:

help	net	bags
ten	pop	fun
ran	hot	little
sun		

long-vowel words:

sale	bikes	came
lined	chased	home
gate	five	
rode	cute	

Cecee's Cake ....page 14
hard c words:

come	cone	cow
cake	cane	cage
coat	curb	

soft c words:

center	cent	city
circus	cider	cell
cement	circle	

Get in the Game ....page 15
1. gym   8. gate
2. gym   9. gate
3. gate   10. gym
4. gym   11. gym
5. gate   12. gate
6. gate   13. gate
7. gym   14. gym

The Scary Story Club...page 16
Scary Story Club Meeting This Thursday!

Bring a spooky scarf and your best fake scabs! The Scary Story Club will meet at Steve's house on Tuesday. Stop by to share your stories.

Spin a tale about scary spiders or monsters that turn students to stone.

Don't be shy to speak! Share your tale and cast a spell. Stay to hear all of the stories! It would be a shame to miss this special meeting.

Danger! ....page 17
1. dr, dream   8. br, bread
2. gr, gray   9. fr, fruit
3. tr, train   10. tr, trip
4. gr, grain   11. cr, crack
5. br, bright   12. dr, dragon
6. dr, drops   13. cr, cross
7. br, brown   14. br, brave

Flickering Flames ....page 18
1. bloom   4. slide
2. cloudy   5. planet
3. glue   6. flames
7.–10. Answers will vary.

Spring Flowers.............page 19
1. thr   6. spl   11. thr
2. spl   7. scr   12. str
3. spr   8. spr   13. thr
4. spl   9. str   14. str
5. scr   10. scr

Summer Break............page 20
1. nd   5. nt   9. nt
2. nd   6. nd   10. nk
3. nk   7. nt   11. nt
4. nt   8. nk   12. nd

Riding the Pony Express...................page 21
1. past   7. fast
2. wild   8. cold
3. rest   9. lamp
4. told   10. dust
5. west   11. jump
6. risk   12. task

Cheer for the Team.....page 23
ea words:

team	leave	east
teach	meal	mean
real	heat	

ee words:

feel	seen
free	teeth

1.–4. Answers will vary.

The "O" Team ....page 24
oa words may include any six of these:

boat(s)	coat(s)	loan(s)
float(s)	bloat(s)	
groan(s)	coast	

ow words may include any six of these:

snow	flow
grow	grown
row	blown
glow	flown

Autumn Leaves ....page 25
1. au   6. au   11. au
2. oo   7. oo   12. au
3. ew   8. oo   13. ew
4. ew   9. ew   14. oo
5. au   10. oo

Crawling Along...........page 26
1. aw   8. ou
2. ow   9. aw
3. aw   10. ow
4. ou   11. aw
5. ow   12. aw
6. aw   13. ou
7. ou   14. aw

 Answer Key

An Eye on the Pie........page 27
1. die
2. flies
3. thief
4. tie
5. shield
6. lie
7. field
8. chief

pie words:
die   tie
flies   lie

shield words:
thief   field
shield   chief

The Pony and the Fly ..page 28
y sounds like i:
try   shy   my
fly   eye   by
why   dry   fry

y sounds like e:
only   very   any
pretty lady   tiny
baby   happy   many

Message in a Bottle ....page 30
Dear Friend,

This is my last chance. It is a shame I shall never see the treasure chest and all its gold. But be of good cheer. Your luck is about to change.

In this bottle is a chart that will show you the way to our sunken ship. Once it sailed proudly on the sea, but now it is down on the bottom with the shells. The chest is in the captain's room. A big chain is around it. The chain is closed with a lock. The key is here for you. Shake the bottle and it should come out.

Look sharp and keep your mouth shut or your time as a rich man will be short. It makes me happy to share this with you and your children. Others in the crew may still be alive. They might chase you if they find out you have the gold, but keep your chin up. I know you will win in the end.

Our Field Trip.......................31
1. third
2. think
3. whales
4. them
5. while
6. Thunder
7. than
8. Then
9. whale
10. There
11. why
12. three
13. throw
14. They
15. Where
16. That
17. thank
18. what
19. The

Space Safari...............page 33
1. sh, spaceship
2. sh, shook
3. Ch, Chills
4. sh, pushing
5. Wh, What
6. ch, charts
7. ch, chosen
8. sh, splashed

More Rhyming Riddles ....page 34
1. long gong
2. strong song
3. king ring
4. swing sting
5. math bath
6. sloth cloth
7. clang fang
8. stinger bringer
9. path bath

The Laughing Elephant.................page 35
1. elephant
2. alphabet, phone
3. tough
4. photograph
5. enough, cough
6. laugh
7. rough
8. nephew

A Whale of a Puzzle ....page 36
across:
3. chase
5. them
6. change
8. cough
11. show
14. watch
15. there
16. three
17. rough

down:
1. ring
2. where
3. chips
4. school
5. tough
7. enough
9. father
10. white
11. sheet
12. other
13. laugh
14. what

Starry, Starry Night ......page 38
1. jar
2. tar
3. star
4. scar
5. hard
6. yard
7. bark
8. car
9. park
10. mark
11. dark
12. part
13. shark

Lucky Clover ....page 39
1. ur
2. ir
3. or
4. er
5. ur
6. or
7. ir
8. ur
9. er
10. morning
11. porch
12. hurt
13. shirt
14. turn

Roy's Coins ....page 40
oi and oy words:
Roy('s)   toil   toys
join   soil   joy
coin(s)   boil   moist
boys   point   spoil
enjoy   foil   avoid

Special Vowels ....page 41
1. oil
2. noise
3. shout
4. owl
5. plow
6. toys
7. crowd
8. pound
9. boils
10. soil
11. point
12. mouth
13. tower
14. boy

Knock Knock..............page 42
1. ripe
2. nice
3. run
4. note
5. never
6. real
7. rake
8. nest
9. next
10. nap
11. ran
12. net
13. needle

A Brave Knight ....page 43
In order of apperance:
night; gh circled
knight; kn and gh circled
signed; g circled
knew; k circled
high; gh circled
light; gh circled
gnats; g circled
climb; b circled
sword; w circled

Summer Camp ....page 44
words with silent letters:
would   gnats   enough
knew   fight   caught
knife   wrist   wrote
flashlight wrap   write
climb   taught

Chasing Jojo..............page 45
1. walked, walking
2. enjoyed, enjoying
3. burned, burning
4. cleaned, cleaning
5. coughed, coughing
6. danced, dancing
7. brushed, brushing
8. chewed, chewing
9. covered
10. crashing
11. asked
12. calling
13. boiling
14. dressed

Tall, Taller, Tallest ....page 46
1. happier, happiest
2. stronger, strongest
3. greener, greenest
4. shorter, shortest
5. kinder, kindest
6. curlier, curliest
7. newer, newest
8. tougher, toughest
9. quicker, quickest
10. older, older
11. greatest
12. longer
13. fastest
14. quieter

Helpful Suffixes ....page 47
1. colorful, colorless
2. hopeful, hopeless
3. powerful, powerless
4. thoughtful, thoughtless
5. useful, useless
6. careful, careless
7. helpful, helpless
8. harmful, harmless
9. thankful, thankless
10. fearful, fearless
11. colorful
12. harmless
13. hopeful
14. fearful
15. thoughtful

Artful Endings ....page 48
1. lucky
2. sticky
3. cloudy
4. squeaky
5. frosty
6. slowly
7. quickly
8. weekly
9. softly
10. friendly
11. loudly
12. stinky
13. sleepy
14. quietly
15. really

Bookish Benita ....page 49
1. childish
2. lovable
3. doable
4. reddish
5. bookish
6. boyish
7. greenish
8. enjoyable
9. likable
10. playable

Review and Recite......page 50
1. do
2. paid
3. done
4. call
5. happy
6. made
7. write
8. able
9. means not heated
10. means to arrange again
11. means to make again
12. means not cooked
13. means not tied
14. means to run again

Tonight's Preview ....page 51
1. pre
2. dis
3. pre
4. pre
5. dis
6. dis
7. pre
8. dis
9. dis

Don't Oversleep! ....page 52
1. overdo
2. overuse
3. mistreat
4. misspell
5. oversleep
6. misuse
7. misunderstand
8. overbake
9. miscount
10. mishear
11. overpay
12. mislabel
13. overflow
14. misnamed
15. overeat

Super Sleuth ....page 53
1. shortest
2. newer
3. quickly
4. colorful
5. thoughtless
6. fearful
7. cloudy
8. boyish
9. lovable
10. redo
11. overuse
12. misspell
13. unture
14. disappear

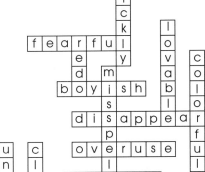

Birthday Surprise ....page 55
1. gifts
2. dishes
3. dimes
4. peaches
5. pitches
6. glasses
7. dresses
8. lakes
9. lights
10. hills
11. shells
12. boxes
13. foxes
14. races
15. wheels
16. brushes

Bunches of Bugs ....page 56
1. axes
2. benches
3. birds
4. boxes
5. cows
6. coaches
7. classes
8. parts
9. pigs
10. dresses
11. horses
12. dishes
13. snakes
14. watches

Special Cases ....page 57
1. children
2. women
3. deer
4. teeth
5. feet
6. geese
7. sheep
8. moose
9. men
10. mice

Bear's Bed ....page 58
1. truck's windows
2. Marina's game
3. bear's fur
4. Chandra's bag
5. boy's gloves
6. monkey's tail
7. birds' wings
8. dentists' office
9. books' covers
10. scouts' tents
11. students' homework
12. players' field

The Cows' Escape.......page 59
1. dog's
2. boys'
3. cats'
4. rooms'
5. Mary's
6. cars'
7. school's
8. girls'
9. neighbor's
10. teacher's
11. guests'
12. students'

An Afternoon Daydream..............page 60
1. after noon
2. air plane
3. camp fire
4. foot step
5. butter milk
6. grand father
7. keyboard
8. moutaintop
9. classroom
10. daydream
11. homework
12. carefree
13. daylight
14.–15. Answers will vary.

Answer Key

Little Mountain Town...page 61
1. bedroom
2. downstairs
3. Outside
4. seashore
5. seashells
6. sidewalk
7. baseball
8. fireworks
9. everything

Skill Drill.....................page 62
1. would not
2. we have
3. did not
4. that is (or that was)
5. we would (or we had)
6. he will
7. has not
8. she is (or she was)
9. will not
10. I have
11. They would
12. does not
13. We have
14. will not
15. I am

Contraction Action .....page 63
1. That's
2. There's
3. He's
4. We'll
5. They'll
6. Aren't
7. What's
8. won't
9. can't
10. He's
11. aren't
12. can't
13. weren't
14. You'll

Take Note.....................page 64
1. re/write
2. re/fill
3. un/tie
4. soft/ly
5. pre/test
6. thought/ful
7. sleep/less
8. dis/like
9. rain/y
10. neat/ly
11. over/hear
12. fast/er

Look It Up.....................page 65
1. fe/ver
2. ba/by
3. se/cret
4. ze/bra
5. la/bel
6. spi/der
7. ti/ny
8. si/lent
9. mu/sic
10. car/toon
11. thir/teen
12. gar/den
13. um/pire
14. win/dow
15. num/ber

Separating Syllables...page 66
1. bat/ter
2. bud/dy
3. um/pire
4. se/cret
5. un/do
6. ti/ny
7. no/thing
8. si/lent
9. spi/der
10. mis/place
11. ar/row
12. pre/view
13. mail/box
14. thir/teen
15. ti/tle
16. la/ter
17. tip/toe
18. ze/bra

Synonym Means the Same.....................page 67
1. silent
2. leave
3. task
4. shake
5. look
6. smile
7. woods
8. dog
9. fall
10. happy
11. begin
12. lovely
13. fast
14. muddy

Antonym Is the Opposite ....page 68
1. slow
2. hard
3. light
4. day
5. down
6. over
7. girl
8. hate
9. evening
10. wet
11. little
12. fresh
13. cold

A Pair of Pears ....page 69
1. aunt
2. bee
3. bear
4. beet
5. blew
6. brakes
7. buy
8. sell
9. new
10. not
11. clothes
12. dear
13. ate
14. I
15. four
16. here
17. heard
18. whole
19. no
20. knight

The Bare Bear..............page 70
1. knew
2. not
3. no
4. knight
5. one
6. hour
7. pair
8. piece
9. write
10. rode
11. sent
12. There
13. toe
14. wait
15. aunt

Same but Different ......page 71
1. feed
2. fed
3. fuzz
4. give
5. how
6. know
7. tuned
8. bead
9. bed
10. hive
11. found
12. know
13. bear
14. cow
15. hear
16. glows

Brain Busters ....page 72
1. tail
2. give
3. never
4. sail
5. near
6. harm
7. sad
8. you're
9. story
10. shout

Write the Order ....page 73
1. around
   buy
   clothes
   does
   eight
   fire
2. give
   head
   itself
   just
   keep
   lamb
3. mouth
   night
   pair
   quick
   round
   second
4. though
   until
   very
   yellow
   zipper

Ready, Set, March! .....page 74
1. back
2. pen
3. scream
4. fair
5. car
6. king
7. save
8. wet
9. day
10. cast
11. sand, send, soft
12. gave, germ, gum
13. ram, ride, rode
14. mask, most, must
15. batter, bedding, black

Putting It Together ......page 75
1. The book was on the top shelf.
2. They sailed a boat around the lake.
3. She put her bike away carefully.
4. He bought new shoes.
5. They had a picnic at the park.
6. The princess danced with the prince.

Matching Meanings..............76
1. F
2. D
3. E
4. G
5. B
6. C
7. A
8. L
9. I
10. J
11. H
12. K

0-7424-2833-8 *Reading for Every Child: Phonics*